ISSUES OF CHURCH, STATE, & RELIGIOUS LIBERTIES
Whose Freedom, Whose Faith?

RELIGION & MODERN CULTURE
Title List

ISSUES OF CHURCH, STATE, & RELIGIOUS LIBERTIES
Whose Freedom, Whose Faith?

by Kenneth McIntosh, M.Div.,
and Marsha McIntosh

Mason Crest Publishers
Philadelphia

Mason Crest Publishers Inc.
370 Reed Road
Broomall, Pennsylvania 19008
(866) MCP-BOOK (toll free)

First printing
1 2 3 4 5 6 7 8 9 10

Library of Congress Cataloging-in-Publication Data

McIntosh, Kenneth, 1959–
    Issues of church, state & religious liberties : whose freedom, whose faith? /
    by Kenneth R. McIntosh and Marsha L. McIntosh.
       p. cm. — (Religion and modern culture)
    Includes index.
    ISBN 1-59084-973-6   ISBN 1-59084-970-1 (series)
    1. Freedom of religion. 2. Church and state. 3. Christianity and politics.
    I. McIntosh, Marsha. II. Title. III. Series.
    BV741.M35 2006
    323.44'2'0973—dc22
                                                    2005015617

Produced by Harding House Publishing Service, Inc.
www.hardinghousepages.com
Interior design by Dianne Hodack.
Cover design by MK Bassett-Harvey.
Printed in India.

CONTENTS

INTRODUCTION

by Dr. Marcus J. Borg

You are about to begin an important and exciting experience: the study of modern religion. Knowing about religion—and religions—is vital for understanding our neighbors, whether they live down the street or across the globe.

Despite the modern trend toward religious doubt, most of the world's population continues to be religious. Of the approximately six billion people alive today, around two billion are Christians, one billion are Muslims, 800 million are Hindus, and 400 million are Buddhists. Smaller numbers are Sikhs, Shinto, Confucian, Taoist, Jewish, and indigenous religions.

Religion plays an especially important role in North America. The United States is the most religious country in the Western world: about 80 percent of Americans say that religion is "important" or "very important" to them. Around 95 percent say they believe in God. These figures are very different in Europe, where the percentages are much smaller. Canada is "in between": the figures are lower than for the United States, but significantly higher than in Europe. In Canada, 68 percent of citizens say religion is of "high importance," and 81 percent believe in God or a higher being.

The United States is largely Christian. Around 80 percent describe themselves as Christian. In Canada, professing Christians are 77 percent of the population. But religious diversity is growing. According to Harvard scholar Diana Eck's recent book *A New Religious America*, the United States has recently become the most religiously diverse country in the world. Canada is also a country of great religious variety.

Fifty years ago, religious diversity in the United States meant Protestants, Catholics, and Jews, but since the 1960s, immigration from Asia, the Middle East, and Africa has dramatically increased the number of people practicing other religions. There are now about six million Muslims, four million Buddhists, and a million Hindus in the United States. To compare these figures to two historically important Protestant denominations in the United States, about 3.5 million are Presbyterians and 2.5 million are Episcopalians. There are more Buddhists in the United States than either of these denominations, and as many Muslims as the two denominations combined. This means that knowing about other religions is not just knowing about people in other parts of the world—but about knowing people in our schools, workplaces, and neighborhoods.

Moreover, religious diversity does not simply exist between religions. It is found within Christianity itself:

• There are many different forms of Christian worship. They range from Quaker silence to contemporary worship with rock music to traditional liturgical worship among Catholics and Episcopalians to Pentecostal enthusiasm and speaking in tongues.

- Christians are divided about the importance of an afterlife. For some, the next life—a paradise beyond death—is their primary motive for being Christian. For other Christians, the afterlife does not matter nearly as much. Instead, a relationship with God that transforms our lives this side of death is the primary motive.
- Christians are divided about the Bible. Some are biblical literalists who believe that the Bible is to be interpreted literally and factually as the inerrant revelation of God, true in every respect and true for all time. Other Christians understand the Bible more symbolically as the witness of two ancient communities—biblical Israel and early Christianity—to their life with God.

Christians are also divided about the role of religion in public life. Some understand "separation of church and state" to mean "separation of religion and politics." Other Christians seek to bring Christian values into public life. Some (commonly called "the Christian Right") are concerned with public policy issues such as abortion, prayer in schools, marriage as only heterosexual, and pornography. Still other Christians name the central public policy issues as American imperialism, war, economic injustice, racism, health care, and so forth. For the first group, values are primarily concerned with individual behavior. For the second group, values are also concerned with group behavior and social systems. The study of religion in North America involves not only becoming aware of other religions but also becoming aware of differences within Christianity itself. Such study can help us to understand people with different convictions and practices.

And there is one more reason why such study is important and exciting: religions deal with the largest questions of life. These questions are intellectual, moral, and personal. Most centrally, they are:

- What is real? The religions of the world agree that "the real" is more than the space-time world of matter and energy.
- How then shall we live?
- How can we be "in touch" with "the real"? How can we connect with it and become more deeply centered in it?

This series will put you in touch with other ways of seeing reality and how to live.

Chapter 1

CHURCH & STATE
Freedom & Conflicts

RELIGION & MODERN CULTURE

The *Santero*, his wrinkled face dark against his white ceremonial cap, looks down at the young man who kneels before him. The man has had a string of bad luck lately: his business went bad, his wife left him. He wonders out loud, "Perhaps I have offended one of the deities."

The Santero takes a chicken, washes it carefully, and holds it over the head of the young man. The old man prays for good health, spiritual and material abundance, and pardon for any sin the younger man may have committed. The Santero picks up a sacred coconut and places it to his ear. After a few moments of silence, he smiles. The *Orisha* (a supernatural being) has communicated his pleasure. The young man stands and begins turning slowly in circles as the Santero blesses him, circling the man, still holding the chicken. Then, the Santero takes a razor-sharp knife and quickly slices the throat of the chicken.

Sacrifice is part of the religion outsiders call Santeria. Those who practice this faith that is rooted in ancient African and Caribbean colonies call it simply "Religion" or "the Religion." The idea of sacrificing fowl in a worship service may make you uncomfortable. Most likely, however, you have no objection to a chicken served on your plate for dinner.

In 1992, members of a Santeria congregation in Hialeah, Florida, wanted to build a church. Some citizens of Hialeah were alarmed and attended city hall meetings to argue their case against the group. Some of the opponents were from animal rights groups. Others were *conservative* Christians who considered Santeria *blasphemous*. They warned that God would punish the city if it allowed this group to build a church. Eventually, the case went as far as the Supreme Court. The judges finally ruled that Hialeah could not prevent the Santerians from building their church. It would be a violation of religious liberty.

The case of the Santerian church and the city of Hialeah, Florida, represents just one out of thousands of issues concerning religious freedom in the United States and Canada. As North America grows increasingly diverse in its religions, conflicts over faith issues arise more often. Citizens have widely varying religious beliefs—or no religious beliefs. As the religious world becomes broader and more complex, it becomes more difficult to please everyone. Almost all citizens of the United States and Canada believe in religious liberty. Yet it can become difficult to make room for everyone's rights. Whose freedom and whose faith should government guard?

As Professor Marcus Borg says in the introduction to this book, religions answer the most important questions in life. Where did we come from? What makes behavior right or wrong? Is there a divine plan for this world? For many people, religious beliefs are absolute: if God created human beings for a purpose, then fulfilling that purpose is the most important thing they can do. Since religion is vital to many citizens' lives, differing religious views can cause deep conflicts.

At the same time, spiritual beliefs can lead to a sense of tolerance. Most religions have some form of the teaching "love your neighbor."

GLOSSARY

blasphemous: Expressing or involving disrespect for God or sacred things.

conservative: Unwilling to consider new ideas, while favoring traditional ways of doing things.

fundamentalists: Those who follow a religious or political belief based on a literal interpretation of and strict adherence to a doctrine.

secular: Having to do with the nonreligious world.

Christianity, Judaism, and Islam teach that God created mortals with the free will to make their own choices in the world. People of faith have argued that God's gift of freedom to humanity should cause spiritual people to allow freedom to others.

A ROUGH START FOR RELIGIOUS FREEDOM

From the time European settlers arrived in North America, there have been conflicts over the role of religion in the life of its people. Many colonists came to the New World for religious reasons. The Puritans, for example, came in 1629 to establish a "heavenly city." They created a deeply religious and creative culture that has had a lasting effect on the

RELIGION & MODERN CULTURE

"Legislature should 'make no law respecting an establishment of religion, or prohibiting the free exercise thereof,' thus building a wall of separation between Church and State."

—*Thomas Jefferson, letter to Connecticut Baptists*

United States. Unfortunately, they were as religiously intolerant as the English Church from which they sought to escape. They were unforgiving of differing beliefs in the Massachusetts Bay colony. The Puritans are famous for the witch trials of 1692, during which they accused many women and men of being witches or warlocks. The Puritan government arrested, tortured, and burned alleged witches and warlocks. Colonists were so shocked by the horrors of the witch trials that these events moved the colonies toward greater religious freedom.

THE FIRST AMENDMENT TO THE U.S. CONSTITUTION

As people with different backgrounds began to settle in North America, more became opposed to the idea of a church established by the government. British colonies such as Rhode Island and Pennsylvania truly had religious liberty. Influenced by freethinkers such as William Penn and Thomas Paine, the colonists began to want more than just religious liberty. They wanted to make their own laws—to govern themselves.

Shortly before declaring their independence, the thirteen colonies began to write constitutions. These documents formed rules for how each government would function once they became states. When colonists adopted the U.S. Constitution in 1787 (it was ratified by the individual colonies by 1789), it limited the powers of the national government. Many citizens felt, however, that it was not clear enough on specific civil and religious liberties. Consequently, James Madison prepared

"Proclaim liberty throughout the land to all the inhabitants."

—Leviticus 25:10

the ten amendments (additions to the Constitution) also known as the Bill of Rights. The first amendment guarantees the people of the United States religious liberty: "Congress shall make no law respecting an establishment of religion, or prohibiting the free exercise thereof." After centuries of hardships caused by nations that imposed religious beliefs on their citizens in Europe, the people wanted religion to be a matter of personal choice rather than state rule. In the eighteenth century, Bible-believing Christians were among the strongest supporters of this separation between church and state.

THE CANADIAN CHARTER OF RIGHTS & FREEDOMS

After the thirteen colonies became the United States of America, thousands of English loyalists fled to Canada. Coming from the thirteen colonies, they knew firsthand the troubles that came from a government closely tied to the church.

While Canada has its own religious freedom issues, they are less common than they are in their neighbor to the south. The United States is unusual among developed nations for the fervency of its citizens' faith. Therefore, citizens debate religious freedom issues more often in the United States than in Canada.

Canadians adopted the Charter of Rights and Freedoms in 1982. Article two of the charter states:

Everyone has the following fundamental freedoms: (a) freedom of conscience and religion; (b) freedom of thought, belief, opinion,

MAJOR RELIGIOUS DIFFERENCES BETWEEN CANADA & THE UNITED STATES

According to religioustolerance.org, Canada is much less religious than the United States. In a 1999 survey, Canadian adults who attend regular religious services number about 20 percent of the population; in the United States they number around 40 percent. The percentage of Roman Catholic adults in the United States (28 percent) is much lower than in Canada (42 percent). However, Canadian citizens tend to support some political positions that go against the teachings of the Catholic Church. The main Protestant denominations in Canada are the United Church of Canada and the Anglican Church of Canada—both of which tend to be theologically liberal. By contrast, the largest Protestant denomination in the United States is the Southern Baptist Church, which tends to be conservative.

and expression including freedom of the press and other media of communication; (c) freedom of peaceful assembly, and (d) freedom of association.

TENSIONS REGARDING THE LIMITS OF GOVERNMENT & RELIGION IN THE UNITED STATES

Some U.S. citizens believe government is "prohibiting the free exercise" of their religion. Gary Bauer, the director of the Washington, D.C.–based Campaign for Working Families, is speaking out against what he believes is a war on Christian faith in society. He alleges public schools have been the source of some of the worst forms of discrimination. A number of these issues involve Christmas activities. In December of 2004, a New Jersey school district banned Christmas carols, the administration warned teachers in a Florida school not to have Christmas decorations, and other schools did not allow the exchange of Christmas cards. Simply saying "Merry Christmas" was taboo in some cases. Matt Staver of Liberty Council, a legal group, says to allow only the *secular* expression of Christmas is showing animosity, not neutrality. He believes Christmas is constitutional and feels government needs to respect it as a part of America's heritage of faith.

Other citizens, including some religious believers, are concerned that the state is establishing religion. Members of the Baptist Joint Committee do not want the U.S. government's money going to church-based groups. Baptist pastor Charles G. Adams spoke out against President Bush's desire to give money to religious institutions such as church-based drug treatment programs: "To mingle government funds with church funds is to entangle the church with government—and to control the church by government."

The struggle to maintain separation of church and state has been a long, continuing process in North America. In some cases, the U.S. government has not allowed the practices of religious minorities. The government has prohibited the religious rituals of Native Americans, Cubans worshipping African deities, and *fundamentalists* handling deadly serpents. Such cases test the limits of church and state separation.

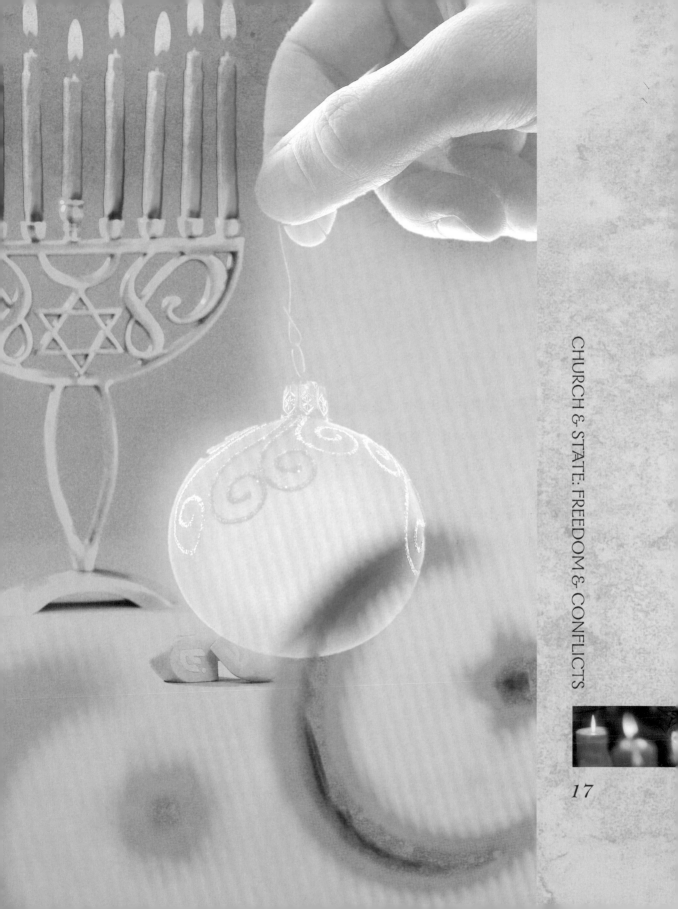

Chapter 2

OUTLAWED RELIGIOUS CEREMONIES

"Thin moustache glistening over white teeth . . . [a young Indian man] . . . abandons himself to the rhythm of the drum. His dark eyes close and his bandanna wrapped head falls back; he opens his throat in song." Nancy Redwine, writer for the *Santa Cruz Sentinel* Web site, uses these words to describe a film documentary by Ismana Carney titled *Iron Lodge. Iron Lodge* tells the story of how ritual and ceremony bring healing to the lives of American Indian prisoners in California.

A Native American man shares his experiences in the film. He grew up in foster homes and orphanages. It was not until he ended up in prison that he came to understand his Indian culture. In prison, he connected with his spiritual heritage of dancing, drumming, and ritual.

The film also tells how countless Indians in prison have grown up on the streets. Many Native prisoners have no connection to their spiritual or cultural traditions until they come to prison. Connecting to their spiritual roots has made dramatic changes in the lives of a number of these men. According to the warden at Solano prison, "The circles have a calming effect on the entire prison population. We may have 80 Indians participating in a ceremony, but there might be 1,500 listening."

Native Americans have not always had the opportunity to practice their religion so openly. The fight for religious freedom has been a long, hard journey.

NATIVE AMERICAN RELIGIOUS RITUALS PROHIBITED

For hundreds of years, Native Americans have fought to practice their *traditional* religions. The U.S. government realized that if it discouraged tribal religious activity, it could more easily put down tribal political activity as well—so it forced Christianity on the Indians. The government hoped that if it could destroy the Native traditions, the Indians would melt into white Christian society. As a result, authorities outlawed spiritual dances such as the Ghost Dance and the Sun Dance. The military slaughtered Sioux Ghost Dancers at Wounded Knee and arrested Ghost Dancers in Oklahoma.

Beginning in 1886, federal Indian agents tried to outlaw peyote, a cactus containing a narcotic used in Native worship. Over the years, state governments continued to outlaw Native American religious customs. California authorities arrested three Navajo men in 1962 for violating laws against the distribution of peyote—but two years later, the California Supreme Court declared prohibiting the use of peyote was a

GLOSSARY

aboriginal: Relating to the earliest inhabitants of a region.

indigenous: Native to a region.

traditional: Having to do with beliefs and behaviors established by ancestors and passed along from generation to generation.

violation of religious freedom. Federal authorities have since protected the use of peyote for religious purposes. Nonetheless, some states continued to list peyote as a drug subject to state laws.

To protect Native American religions, Congress passed the American Indian Religious Freedom Act (AIRFA) in 1978. It states:

> It shall be the policy of the United States to protect and preserve for American Indians their inherent right of freedom to believe, express, and exercise the traditional religions of the American Indian, Eskimo, Aleut, and Native Hawaiians.

Unfortunately, the law does not say how authorities should enforce it. Even after Congress passed AIRFA, many Indians ended up in prison for practicing their traditional spirituality. After continued conflicts between government policy and state drug laws, Congress added to the act in 1994. The amendment allows for Indian use, possession, or transportation of peyote when for religious, ceremonial purposes. The federal and state governments may not make laws against such an act.

> *"The legitimate powers of government extend to such acts only as are injurious to others. But it does me no injury for my neighbor to say there are twenty gods or no god. It neither picks my pocket, nor breaks my leg."*
>
> —*Thomas Jefferson*

NATIVE RELIGION ISSUES IN CANADA

In Canada, as in the United States, *indigenous* people have struggled for religious freedom. The government suppressed Native spirituality and outlawed many ceremonies. Spiritual leaders could face up to thirty years in prison if found practicing their traditional rituals. According to the Web site Indian and Northern Affairs Canada, the state considered *Aboriginal* people to be "wards and children of the State."

In 1876, Canadians passed the first version of the Indian Act, a collection of previous Indian laws. Almost yearly, authorities made amendments to the act. In 1884, the Canadian government issued an amendment prohibiting sacred ceremonies. In 1895, other laws followed that prohibited Native spiritual dances. In 1914, the Canadian government barred western Indians from wearing "Aboriginal costume" at any dance or show without official permission. In 1933, an amendment stated that Indians could not participate in ceremonial events no matter what they were wearing; Aboriginals could only dance if a government official gave special permission. The Canadian government revised the Indian Act in 1951, and this revision allowed dancing and participation in exhibitions, shows, and other special events. Not until 1982 did Canadian Natives attain a promise of religious freedom when the Canadian government passed the Charter of Rights and Freedoms.

"Religious experiences, which are as real as life to some, may be incomprehensible to others."
—*William O. Douglas*

SANTERIA & THE ISSUE OF ANIMAL SACRIFICE

As mentioned in chapter 1, Santeria is another religious practice that has suffered from government attempts to limit its members' worship. Because Cuban slave masters prohibited African forms of worship, their slaves craftily mixed their native religion—Western African Yoruba belief—with Catholicism. Slaves went through the actions of worshipping Catholic saints—Santa Barbara, San Miguel, and so on—but inwardly they were honoring their African Orishas, minor deities who control human destiny. Thus, in Santeria, the saints became one with the Orishas. Santeria spread to the New World from these West African slaves. Immigration of Cubans to the U.S. mainland greatly increased the practice of this religion in Florida and New York.

When the city of Hialeah tried to outlaw Santeria, it was largely because of its practice of animal sacrifice. The New Religious Movements Web site explains: "When religion requires the sacrifice of an animal . . . it is killed quickly and with as little pain as possible." The participants of the sacrifice usually eat the meat. If the sacrifice is part of a ritual cleansing, the practitioner throws the meat away.

The city of Hialeah was concerned that the disposal of the sacrifices was a public health hazard. In the early nineties, the city passed several laws prohibiting the killing of animals in public rituals or ceremonies. Santeria members felt targeted by the law, so the president of a local Santeria church decided to fight the restrictions. He claimed that animal sacrifices were a basic and important part of the religion; to prohibit their practice denied Santerians their First Amendment right to religious freedom. The Supreme Court agreed.

SNAKE HANDLING: STATES TRY TO PROTECT CHURCH MEMBERS

George Hensley preached loud and long at the Church of God, in Cleveland, Tennessee. He read from the Bible passage, Mark chapter 16: "And these signs shall follow them that believe. . . . They shall take up serpents; and if they drink any deadly thing, it shall not hurt them." As he spoke, several men jumped up from the congregation and dumped a box of snakes in front of the pulpit. Without missing a beat, preaching the whole time, Hensley reached down, picked up the snakes, and finished his sermon.

Snake handling is another religious practice banned in the United States. Most people believe the practice started with George Hensley in the hills of Tennessee sometime around 1910, born out of the Pentecostal Holiness Movement. By 1914, snake handling had spread to many Churches of God, which now called themselves the Church of God with Signs Following. By 1928, only a few churches in the Appalachian Mountains continued the practice. However, snake handling revived in the 1940s.

When a snake handler in the Church of God died in 1947, the State of Tennessee officially banned the practice. In the South, five other states (Kentucky, 1940; Georgia, 1941; Virginia, 1947; North Carolina, 1949; Alabama, 1950) also banned snake handling.

After states made these laws, snake handling again faded from public consciousness. Then in 1971, snakebites or strychnine poisoning were the cause of death for three people in Tennessee and Georgia, and Tennessee placed a ban on the snake-handling ritual. The states that banned snake handling denied religious freedom to the snake handlers because of the danger to the church congregation.

Today there are from fifty to one hundred snake-handling churches from Florida to West Virginia to Ohio. West Virginia has no law prohibiting snake handling, but in Tennessee, for example, it is an offense

POLYGAMY IN CANADA

According to religioustolerance.org, an excommunicated group of Latter Day Saints settled in rural British Columbia where they continued to practice polygamy. The Canadian government has recently challenged them on their lifestyle. The attorney general chose not to prosecute them for their crime of bigamy (marrying more than one person at a time). He believed the case would not win because of the Canadian Charter of Rights and Freedoms, which protects religious freedom.

to handle a poisonous snake in such a way as to endanger a person. Kentucky also specifically outlaws snake handling. In Alabama, authorities can prosecute a snake handler under the reckless endangerment laws.

Approximately seventy-seven members of the Church of God with Signs Following have died from snakebites. George Hensley himself died on July 25, 1955, in Florida, from a diamondback snakebite. But the people who practice this faith continue to be convinced that they are following a biblical mandate. For them, snake handling is a vital aspect of their faith. To outlaw it is to restrict their religious freedom.

Polygamy is the custom of having more than one spouse at a time; it usually involves a man having multiple wives. Joseph Smith, the leader of the Church of Jesus Christ of Latter Day Saints (LDS), first introduced the practice of polygamy to the United States in 1830, and married his own second wife in 1835. Joseph Smith kept his many marriages as secret as possible during his lifetime, but some historians believe he had at least thirty-three wives. He also appointed wives for some of the other men of the church.

In 1844, a group split from the LDS church. William Law, the leader, wrote an article in the *Nauvoo Expositor* exposing some of the Mormon's secret practices, including polygamy. Authorities arrested Joseph and his brother Hyrum. While they were in jail, a mob broke in and killed them. Brigham Young then became the leader and continued the practice of polygamy. He had fifty-five wives and fathered fifty-six children.

In 1862, the U.S. government passed the Morrill Anti-Bigamy Law, making it a criminal offence to have multiple marriage partners. The crime was punishable by up to five years in prison and $500 in fines. For many years after this, the LDS church engaged in legal battles with government authorities over polygamy. The state took the citizen rights of LDS members away; they could not vote or hold public office. Authorities put many Mormon men with multiple wives in jail.

The Supreme Court finally ruled that the U.S. government could dissolve the Mormon church. At this point, the church decided to comply with federal law and banned the practice of plural marriage in 1890. The church kicked out some LDS members who rejected this ban. The largest group to leave the church took the name of the Fundamentalist Church of Jesus Christ of the Latter Day Saints, and this group still practices polygamy in the United States and Canada. In 2004, they claimed 10,000 members.

29

In addition to groups that originated with the LDS church, there are a small number of non-Mormon Christian polygamists in the United States who refer to themselves as believers in Christian Patriarchy. These Christian polygamists argue the state has no right to define marriage. Thus, they take multiple wives through religious wedding ceremonies that are not state licensed. Members of the Christian Patriarchy movement are hopeful that the increasing acceptance of nontraditional sexual practices in North America will soon cause governments to legalize polygamy. Christian Patriarchalists have settled near fundamentalist LDS communities, hoping to convert members of the LDS sect to their own form of fundamentalist Christianity.

CITIES REFUSING SPACE FOR HOUSES OF WORSHIP

A church steeple outlined against the skyline is a common sight in Canadian cities. Nowadays, however, it is just as common to see the outlines of mosques and temples on the horizon. Many more Canadians than in the past are claiming to be Hindus, Muslims, Sikhs, and Buddhists. Many of these are recent immigrants.

The United States is also a country of immigrants; yet some U.S. immigrants are finding it difficult to build a place of worship. According to the book *A New Religious America*, "a new immigrant religious community may first encounter its neighbors not over a cup of tea but in a city council or zoning board hearing." Every religious tradition has had to deal with these boards, but new immigrant groups feel the sting of this public examination more severely. Some Americans are not pleased that the United States has become such a nation of religious diversity. There are many stories of insults, assaults, and hatred toward members of minority religions.

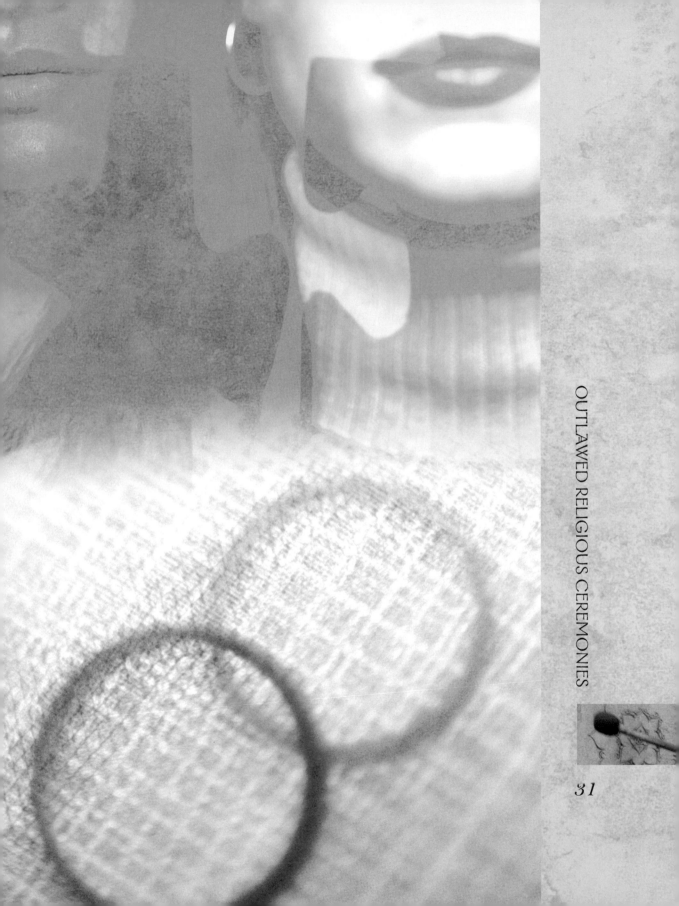

RELIGION & MODERN CULTURE

In the summer of 2000, a group of Muslims in Palos Heights, a suburb of Chicago, made an offer to buy a Reformed Church building that had been on the market for two years. They wanted to convert the space into an Islamic center. When the offer went public, a flurry of town members insisted the town reconsider making the church into a recreation center. During the heated discussions at town hall meetings, one man stated that Islam was an upside-down religion, having its prayers on Friday instead of Sunday. Someone else complained that property values would go down. Another citizen, in support of the center, spoke up to say she would rather raise her children in a town that had religious tolerance than a town with a good recreational facility.

Officials ended up offering the Muslim group $200,000 to walk away from the offer. The Muslims chose to do so. A short time later, the Al Salam Mosque Foundation found out about the issue and filed a suit against the town.

Sikhs in San Diego also wanted to build a place of worship, but the appearance of the new *gurdwara* (temple) was an issue with officials. At first, the city rejected the plan because of the temple's gold domes; city officials said these would not fit in with the "feel" of southern California. However, the city council overturned the decision and allowed the gold domes to join the landscape of the city.

In her book *A New Religious America*, Diana L. Eck points out that in multireligious North America, issues of church and state have become increasingly complex. Public schools are one place where differing cultures and religious beliefs mingle on a daily basis. Sometimes the differences between students are a valued part of the educational experience. Other times, conflicts may ensue. Should schools teach creation along with evolution? Can students wear religious-related clothing or jewelry? Which groups should schools allow to start a religious club on campus?

Chapter 3

RELIGIOUS FREEDOM ISSUES IN EDUCATION

RELIGION & MODERN CULTURE

The first bell rings. Students are scrambling to get last-minute items from lockers. In the midst of this everyday high school mayhem, four or five students are kneeling on the floor by their lockers with heads bowed. This ritual lasts only thirty seconds, and the students are up and off to class. This practice is called 30KD—thirty-second kneel down—and it's going on in high schools across the United States. Tom Sipling, a Pennsylvania youth pastor, is the creator of the idea. Christian high school and middle school students are taking thirty seconds each morning to pray for their teachers, friends, and school administrators. Thousands of students across the country are taking part in this spiritual exercise. Their hope is to have a positive effect on the lives of people around them and to bring prayer—their prayers—back into the public school.

The ban on public school prayer in the United States began in New York State. In 1962, the New York Board of Regents recommended students recite a "neutral" prayer each morning. This would be from no particular religion. Ten parents objected. When parents took the case to the U.S. Supreme Court, a majority of justices agreed with the parents. According to Kathlyn Gay in the book *Church and State*, "The court ruled that state and local governments 'should stay out of the business of . . . official prayers and leave that purely religious function to the people themselves.'"

Many U.S. citizens hold mistaken notions about this Supreme Court ruling. The Supreme Court did not prohibit all forms of prayer from schools; that would deny students freedom of religion. Instead, the Supreme Court outlawed state-sponsored prayer in public schools. The Court said school officials may not organize, order, or participate in student religious activities, including prayer.

At the same time, students are free to pray alone or in groups, as long as these prayers do not bother or deny the rights of others. Student prayer activities must be voluntary and students must lead them. Teenagers who practice 30KD know their religious rights.

In 1995, President Bill Clinton instructed his secretary of education to distribute guidelines for religious expression to all public schools in the United States. These guidelines are still in effect today. In a shortened form, they are as follows:

- Student Prayer—During the school day, students may take part in group or individual prayer.
- Religious Discussion—Students may pray and discuss religion in "informal settings" such as the cafeteria or in the hall.
- Rules for School Administrators and Teachers—Administrators and teachers, in their roles at school, may not encourage or discourage religious activities.

GLOSSARY

Anti-Christ: According to the book of Revelations, an evil world leader who will oppose Christ's followers.

evangelical: Relating to any Protestant Christian church whose members believe in the authority of the Bible and salvation through the personal acceptance of Jesus Christ.

proselytize: To try to convert or recruit others to follow a religion.

Wicca: A pagan religious practice involving nature worship. Some Wiccans call themselves witches.

- Teaching About Religion—Public schools may teach *about* religion, however, they may not ***proselytize*** religion.
- Talking About Religion in School Assignments—Students may express their beliefs in class assignments, artwork, and homework.
- Distributing Religious Literature—Pupils may hand out spiritually based literature to other students. The school has a right to restrict this literature as they do any other literature that is not school related.
- Religious Excusals—Schools may excuse students from lessons that are offensive to them or their parents based on their religion.
- Religious Dress—Students may wear clothing that is religious based such as headscarves and words on clothing.

WWJD

"Nothing in the First Amendment converts our public schools into religion-free zones, or requires all religious expression to be left behind at the school house door."

—*President Bill Clinton, July 12, 1995*

RELIGIOUS CLOTHING—
FAIR FOR SOME IS FAIR FOR ALL

In the late nineties, a number of school-related court cases involved religious clothing. In November of 1998, a high school suspended a student for wearing a T-shirt that displayed a rock band and the numbers 666, a number associated with the *Anti-Christ* in the book of Revelation in the Bible. The American Civil Liberties Union (ACLU) of Rhode Island filed a complaint with the state department of education. A volunteer lawyer for the case said:

> Public schools cannot be in the business of approving a T-shirt about the Lord and banning a T-shirt of a rock band, even one that offends some people. In the process of trying to make schools safe, it is good to get rid of guns. It's not good to suspend common sense or the Bill of Rights.

In October of 1998, a high school in the suburbs of Detroit, Michigan, issued a dress code. The code prohibited students from wearing clothing or jewelry related to youth gangs, white supremacy groups, Satanism, or "Wigga" (they probably meant "*Wicca*"). Pentagrams and pentacles were included in the ban. (A pentagram is a five-pointed star, and a pentacle is a pentagram inside of a circle; both are religious symbols of the Wiccan religion.) The school allowed students to wear other religious symbols in school—such as a cross, Star of David, or a crucifix. An honor student named Crystal, a Wiccan, complained. Several Wiccan groups offered to help the school by giving information to the school authorities and by working to solve the argument. The school refused their help. The ACLU filed a suit against the school on Crystal's behalf. Eventually, the school and ACLU reached an agreement requiring the school district to allow wearing of Wiccan religious symbols. This was a victory not just for Wiccans but also for other religious minorities across the country.

Other cases of Wiccan students experiencing discrimination in schools have occurred in the early 2000s. In almost every case, when the student or parents have defended themselves, the school later allowed students to wear their pentagrams and pentacles.

WHO CAN START A RELIGIOUS CLUB?

Schools, parents, and students have also experienced conflicts concerning religious clubs on public school campuses. In a number of cases, school administrators have refused student requests for religious organizations on campus. The nature of these clubs varies. On the one hand, a school denied use of space to a conservative Christian club desiring to pray and study the Bible. On the other hand, schools have disallowed Wiccan clubs formed to help students understand their religion and rituals and to oppose harassment in the school. Although members of these religious clubs differ in their beliefs and practices, the First Amendment permits both of them.

The Equal Access Law, passed in August of 1984, is helpful for religious clubs. The Supreme Court ruled this law constitutional in 1990

WEARING THEIR FAITH

Some schools have rules against wearing hats or other head coverings. An eleven-year-old girl who attended a school in the Muskogee Public School District was suspended twice for wearing a *hijab*—a headscarf worn by devout Muslim women. The school board said that the scarf was "frightening" to other students. The Justice Department filed a lawsuit in March of 2004 and won. The assistant attorney general for civil rights of the Justice Department said, "This settlement reaffirms the principle that public schools cannot require students to check their faith at the schoolhouse door. . . . It is un-American to fear and to hate."

after the case of *Board of Education of Westside Community Schools v. Mergens.* The school involved in the case sponsored several clubs but would not allow a Christian Bible study club. The Supreme Court ruled public schools must allow any club to meet, with certain limitations: attendance is voluntary, students begin the group, school personnel do not sponsor the group, the group is not disruptive, and people from the community do not lead or regularly attend the meetings.

CONTROVERSY OVER FUNDING CATHOLIC SCHOOLS IN ONTARIO, CANADA

Canada has also had its share of struggles with religious issues in public schools. In Ontario, for instance, public funds finance two school systems—the public school and the Roman Catholic school. If a family is Jewish, Muslim, or Protestant and wants to educate their children in their faith, they must pay for their own education. They must also pay taxes that help fund the public and Catholic school systems. Members of other religions feel this is unfair. They would like the same funding. Critics suggest it might be a nice gesture if the Catholic Church considered giving up its funding; this might help members of other religions feel equal.

TEACHING CREATION & EVOLUTION IN PUBLIC SCHOOLS

How do you think human life started? Did a small, ape-like creature evolve into a human being? Or did God fashion the first man, Adam, from the dust of the earth, breathing life into his nostrils and then forming a woman from his side? For more than a thousand years, Europeans understood the beginnings of human life in terms of religious beliefs. The accounts of creation found in the opening chapters of Genesis shaped Western understanding of cosmic and human origins. In the nineteenth century, however, geologists and biologists made important discoveries about the development of life on our planet. At first, religious leaders welcomed these discoveries, but by the end of the nineteenth century, the religious movement known as fundamentalism began to oppose these scientific explanations of life on earth.

In 1925, a dramatic courtroom trial pitted the teaching of evolution against fundamentalist interpretations of the Bible when John Scopes, a

young teacher, included a lesson on evolution in his classroom. This was against the Butler Act, which forbade the teaching of any theory that disagreed with biblical creation. A leading intellectual lawyer, Clarence Darrow, defended Scopes. The prosecutor was a prominent public speaker and outspoken fundamentalist named William Jennings Bryan.

"Our first challenge in America today is simply to open our eyes to these changes, to discover America anew, and to explore the many ways in which the new immigration has changed the religious landscape of our cities and towns, our neighborhoods and schools."

—*Diana L. Eck*, A New Religious America

The jury found Scopes guilty. However, radio stations broadcasted the trial, and many listeners felt Scopes and Darrow were the real winners. Nonetheless, in some school districts, textbooks did not include the theory of evolution until the early 1960s.

By the end of that decade, teaching of evolution had become common in most public schools. Indeed, through the 1960s there seemed to be little opposition to evolution in public educational settings. At the same time, however, conservative Christians became increasingly committed to belief in creationism. The Creation Research Society formed in 1963 and the Institute for Creation Research organized in 1970. These religious institutions attempted to prove their particular interpretation of the Bible through their own peculiar scientific means. They gained few converts outside of *evangelical* and fundamentalist churches but strengthened belief in their doctrines within those circles. The creationist institutes encouraged conservative Christians to push for the teaching of their beliefs in public schools.

The states of Arkansas and Louisiana tried to pass laws that would force educators to teach creationism along with evolution; they did not pass. The courts ruled it was a violation of the First Amendment to teach a religious belief such as creationism in public schools. In the mid-nineties, creationists tried to convince school boards to give equal time to the teaching of "scientific evidence against evolution." This concerned many scientists, and school boards were not convinced.

At the same time, the Catholic Church made an official statement favoring evolution. On October 23, 1996, Pope John Paul II stated, "Fresh knowledge leads to recognition of the theory of evolution as more than just a hypothesis." Pope Pious XII had issued statements discouraging the belief in evolution in 1950, but it appeared Pope John Paul II was altering the previous position of the Catholic Church.

Not all Christians believe the creation–evolution debate is all that important to the basic tenets of Christian faith. Some Christians, including many evangelicals, believe God created life by means of evolution. They have no problem reconciling the biblical account of creation with science.

According to Michael D. Lemonick in *Time* magazine, January 31, 2005, the latest attack on Darwin's theory of evolution comes from "well funded think tanks promoting a theory they call intelligent design, or I.D." Those who teach ID believe the complexity of life on earth shows that an intelligent designer must have created life. The Discovery Institute in Seattle is a think tank promoting I.D. They encourage schools to continue teaching evolution but also to present what I.D. proponents say are scientific criticisms of the theory. Most scientists, however, deny the theory of evolution is flawed. Many in the scientific community believe those who favor I.D. are using their theory as a smoke screen to promote creationist teachings.

A CANADIAN COLLEGE FACES QUESTIONS OF FAIRNESS TO HOMOSEXUALS

Do you think a religious person, trained at a school that disapproves of homosexual behavior, could become a compassionate teacher for gay students? The province of British Columbia, Canada, didn't think so; as

TEACHING EVOLUTION & CREATION— WHAT THE PEOPLE WANT

In 2002, Channel One News, a cable station that broadcasts directly to schools throughout the United States, conducted an online poll of 12,000 schools to determine the attitude of students toward the teaching of origins. The question was: "Which should be taught in school—evolution, creation, or both?" The responses were: Creationism only—31 percent, Evolution only—17 percent, Both Creationism and Evolution—52 percent.

a result, it tried to take away a license to train teachers from Trinity Western University in 1996. Trinity is an evangelical Christian school that disapproves of homosexual behavior, and officials in British Columbia believed teachers trained there would not be sensitive to gay students in public schools. Five years later, Canada's Supreme Court decided in favor of Trinity Western University.

One justice on the Supreme Court bench voted against the decision. She wrote, "A lack of expertise among school staff creates missed opportunities to help lesbian, bisexual, and gay youth before a crisis develops." John Fisher, the director of a Canadian homosexual-rights group, believes Trinity graduates may not be sensitive when counseling homosexual students.

Steven Pearlstein of the *Washington Post* interviewed Trinity students. One Trinity graduate, a high school English and psychology teacher, shared her experience teaching in one of Canada's public high schools. She had to overcome prejudice from her coworkers at first; they knew she had come from a Christian school. Once they realized she was not going to cross the line from teacher to preacher, things were fine. Students now go to her for counseling on how to deal with friends and parents who don't like the fact that they may be gay. This teacher went on to share, "When I have a student who comes to me—and this happened—and says he's finally found a boyfriend, I'm happy for him. I'm happy he's happy; that's it. It's his life."

Schools are not the only public grounds where differing religious and secular views may conflict; issues regarding religious freedoms exist in the business world as well. Employers must decide if they will give employees time off for religious holidays, what to tolerate in the way of religious dress, and whether they should fire someone who refuses to comply with business practices because of religious beliefs.

Chapter 4

RELIGIOUS FREEDOM ISSUES IN BUSINESS

RELIGION & MODERN CULTURE

Seventeen blindfolded men lie on towels in the basement, each one's breathing, slow and deliberate. Incense fills the candlelit room. A single drum beats in the background as a whispery voice from a **shaman** tells the men to imagine an entry point into the earth such as a pond or a spring. The voice then instructs the listeners to go deep into their inner selves and bring out their "power animals" to help them guide their companies into new and successful ventures.

The shaman is Richard Whiteley, who is also a best-selling author and business consultant. His pupils are presidents of companies attending the Young Presidents Organization Conference in Rome. If these business leaders had tried this exercise ten years ago, they probably would have met with ridicule, but today a spiritual movement is happening in the workplace.

Business leaders are not the only ones attending spiritual events like this one. According to a 1999 *Business Week* article by Michelle Conlin, three hundred Xerox employees participated in "vision quests" over a six-year period. The workers, armed with sleeping bags and water bottles, spent time alone with nature for twenty-four hours in the New Mexico desert or the New York Catskills. They were searching for inspiration and direction; their goal was to construct the first digital copier-fax-printer for Xerox. A dozen engineers had a great idea in northern New Mexico during one of these outings. Conlin writes, they saw a "lone, fading Xerox paper carton bobbing in a swamp of old motor oil at the bottom of a pit. They vowed to build a machine that would never end up polluting another dump." Back at the design offices in Rochester, New York, the office staff took part in a Native American talking circle where they slowly passed a rock around. Only the person holding the stone could speak and share ideas. This made more talkative members of the group stop and listen. John F. Elter, the chief engineer in charge of the project, said the undertaking was a real spiritual experience for almost everyone. The result was the design and production of the 265DC, a 97 percent recyclable machine—and one of Xerox's biggest sellers.

BUSINESS SPIRITUALITY

Corporate America is experiencing a spiritual revival; business leaders are bringing spirituality into the workplace. Workers at places such as

GLOSSARY

demonic: Having to do with demons, spiritual beings who work to influence human beings for evil.

shaman: A Native religious leader who acts as a go-between for the spiritual and physical worlds, and who is said to have particular powers, such as prophecy and healing.

Pizza Hut, Taco Bell, and subsidiaries of Wal-Mart are getting in on the sacred. These groups are hiring army-style chaplains from different religions to attend to the spiritual needs of employees. The chaplains are helpful in all kinds of situations ranging from dealing with nervous breakdowns and suicidal threats to making common hospital visits. They even perform weddings and funerals.

Helping employees spiritually is paying off in many ways. Austaco Inc., which owns Pizza Hut and Taco Bell franchises, has greatly reduced their turnover of employees since hiring chaplains; the restaurants have gone from 300 percent turnover to a rate of 125 percent. "In fast-food time, that's like having workers stay on for an eternity," says Michelle Conlin in her article. One Taco Bell employee explains she would not dream of leaving her job for another one that did not have a religious lifeline. She has a husband in prison, a daughter in rehab, and two children to feed at home. Many times, she gets depressed and needs

53

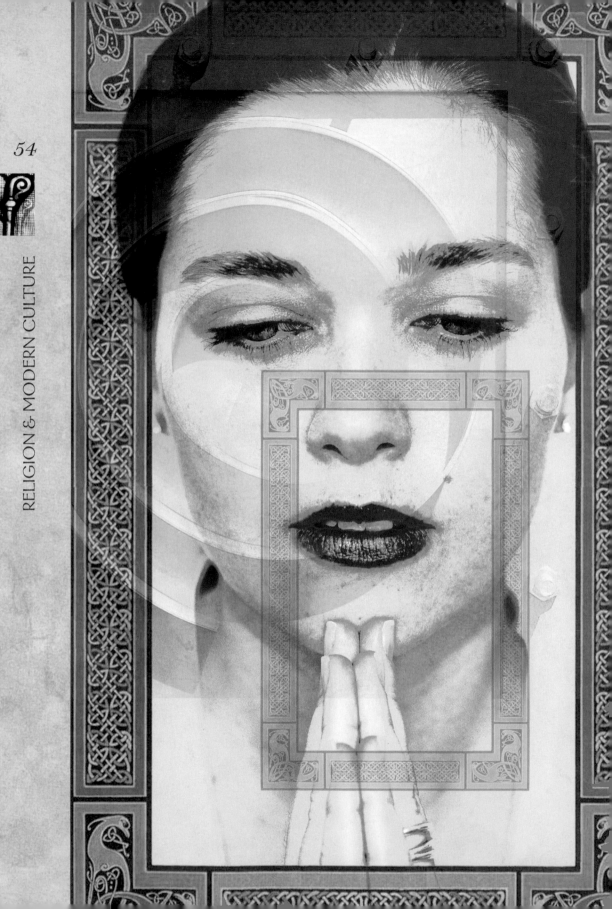

> *"Things which matter most must never be at the mercy of things which matter least."*
>
> —*Johann Wolfgang von Goethe*

desperately to talk with someone. She depends on her weekly meetings with her chaplain. Thirteen other Taco Bells and Pizza Huts around Austin, Texas, are also part of her chaplain's parish.

There are many reasons why spirituality in the workplace is becoming popular. Spiritual programs have a soothing effect on workers. McKinsey & Company in Australia completed research that shows when businesses have programs that use spiritual techniques for employees, workers are more productive, and turnover decreases tremendously. A study done by Ian Mitroff and Elizabeth Denton, *A Spiritual Audit of Corporate America*, showed that when employees considered an organization to be spiritual, they were less fearful, more likely to throw themselves into their jobs, and less likely to go against their values. Sixty percent of those polled for the book thought spirituality at work was beneficial as long as traditional religion is not overemphasized.

The business world has changed in the last twenty years. It is about instant decision making and building relationships with coworkers and business partners. Often, giving people instruction on spiritual matters helps the human side of things, and improving human relations improves the marketplace.

Dr. Paul T. P. Wong, a psychology professor at Canada's Trinity Western University, believes, "The movement to bring spirit and soul to business is no passing fad; it continues to grow. . . . Clearly, something significant and enduring is stirring the corporate world."

But this new spiritual activity also has a possible downside, according to Michelle Conlin's article in *Business Week*. Some people are nervous about the idea of bringing religion into the work arena. Although

56

RELIGION & MODERN CULTURE

WHEN TIMES GET TOUGH,
PEOPLE GET ... RELIGIOUS?

According to Dr. Paul T. P. Wong, research director and counseling professor at Trinity Western University, in British Columbia, Canada, a revival of spirituality is occurring in the workplace for many reasons. Some of these are:

- Workers are afraid they will lose their jobs.
- Workers experience less job satisfaction and more depression and burnout.
- Workers feel more stress because they have to work harder.
- Scandals of immoral behavior at companies (Enron, for example) make both workers and employers feel a need for a moral standard.
- Violence in the workplace, threats of terrorism, and office rage worry both workers and employers.
- Problems in families and schools can disrupt the workplace.

Dr. Wong believes when times are difficult it is natural to turn to spirituality and religion to find answers and peace of mind.

"A business that makes nothing but money is a poor kind of business."

—Henry Ford

page 58, RELIGION & MODERN CULTURE

there is widening acceptance of spirituality in the workplace, at the same time there are conflicts. On one side of the conflict are conservative Christians who fear religious techniques introduced into the workplace may be **demonic**. Other skeptics wonder if spirituality in the workplace is just another management fad to make more money. Because of these concerns, many companies stay away from the spiritual. Unfortunately, the increase of spirituality in business has not eliminated cases of workers being denied their religious freedoms.

RELIGIOUS DISCRIMINATION IN THE WORKPLACE

Under the Civil Rights Act of 1964, the U.S. government requires employers to provide a certain amount of religious freedom in the workplace: freedom that does not cause the employer more than a small amount of cost in time and expense. Sometimes, however, there is tension between employees' right to practice their religion and employers' right to run their business. The Equal Employment Opportunity Commission estimates there has been a 29 percent increase since 1992 in the number of religion-based discrimination charges. The Family Research Council Web site states, "employers routinely . . . deny requests and religious workers are left to deny their faith or lose their jobs." According to the Institute for Public Affairs and the Family Research Council Web sites, the following are cases in which employers have violated workers' religious liberties:

"Few trends could so thoroughly undermine the very foundations of our free society as the acceptance by corporate officials of a social responsibility other than to make as much money for their stockholders as possible."

—*Milton Friedman*

- A twenty-seven-year-old Christian was denied a position as a state trooper when a psychological screening test showed he had strong religious beliefs.
- The New York City Police Department swore in a practicing Sikh as a new officer, but during the eight-week training period, his supervisor requested the man shave his beard and remove his turban. He refused based on his religious beliefs, and his boss fired him. (The Washington, D.C., Metropolitan Police Department allows Sikhs to wear their turbans, as do police forces in Canada.)
- An Orthodox Jew applied to work with a company as a repair technician. He scored high on the employer's test, but his prospective employer said he would not get the job because he would not work on his Sabbath—Saturday. He offered to work on Sunday nights instead. The employer told him Saturday was the busiest day for repair technicians, but later he discovered this was not true.

RELIGION & BUSINESS IN CANADA

Canada has a rich diversity of nationalities and religions. Yet it has a relatively low level of conflict. According to the Foreign Affairs Canada Web site, the workplace is a secular arena. It would be uncommon to find a person who would try to proselytize others in the office. Most Canadian holidays are connected to the Christian religion, but people of other faiths can take time off to celebrate their own holidays as well.

The Workplace Religious Freedom Act (WRFA) is a bill introduced by Senator John Kerry to aid employees in such cases. Legislators have presented the bill repeatedly to the U.S. House and Senate, but it had not been approved as of 2005. Critics claim the bill could give employees excuses to refuse to provide necessary services, harming their employers' businesses or even causing harm to the public.

One major employer in the United States does very well with religious freedom issues: the armed services provide chaplains to assist members of all religions. At the same time, some religions forbid military service. A number of people who oppose war on religious grounds have chosen to leave the United States and emigrate to Canada.

Chapter 5

RELIGIOUS FREEDOM & MILITARY SERVICE

RELIGION & MODERN CULTURE

Marcy Palmer is a soldier—and not just any soldier: the U.S. Army once named her soldier of the year. She is also a chaplain. Her congregation is the Fort Hood Open Circle, a Wiccan group.

When the public became aware that a Wiccan group was meeting at the Fort Hood, Texas, military base, it caused a stir, as described by Diana L. Eck in her book *A New Religious America*. The officer in charge, Captain Gunter, granted the Wiccan group permission to meet and have a chaplain.

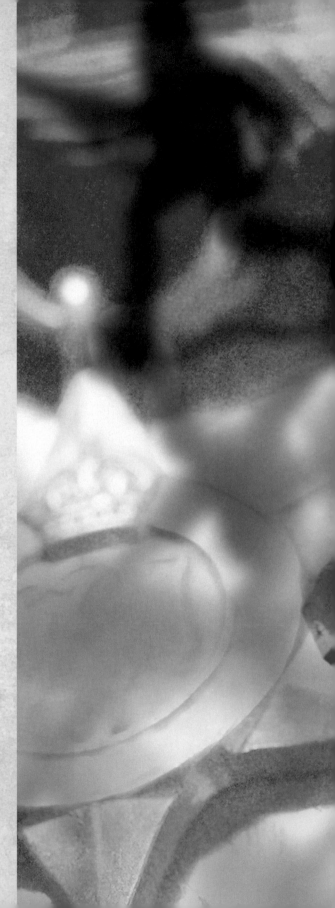

The Department of Defense supported him. Wiccans have been meeting in the army for over twenty years, but this was the first time the media got involved. Captain Gunter's phone rang for six weeks after a local newspaper printed an article about Fort Hood Open Circle. Each time callers asked Captain Gunter about the issue, he informed the caller that the Department of Defense does not judge or choose between religious groups. They provide for the practice of all religions. Army chaplains are prepared to meet the different needs of the men and women at their bases.

GROWING CHANGES IN THE MILITARY

During World War II, Protestant, Catholic, and Jewish men had their faiths printed on their "dog tags," so if they were hurt or dying on the battlefield, a chaplain would know their religious faith. Muslims and Buddhists also served in the armed forces during that war, but the military did not engrave their religion on the backs of their tags. Instead, their tags said "other." Today that has changed.

It took many years of work before men and women of the Islamic faith could worship in a mosque on a military base. The first military mosque opened in 1988 in Virginia at the Norfolk Naval Base. By the year 2000, nine Muslim chaplains had joined the ranks of the U.S. armed forces. The official seal of the chaplains' corps has changed—it now has a crescent along with the Star of David and a cross.

While some religious citizens in the United States and Canada were concerned for their religious rights in the military, others have defended their religious rights *against* service in the military. Some religions teach that killing—even in the armed forces—is contrary to God's will for humanity.

GLOSSARY

conscientious objectors: People who because of their religious convictions will not participate in war or violence.

radicals: Individuals willing to take extreme action to bring about change.

subversive: Intended to undermine or overthrow an institution.

RELIGIOUS OBJECTORS TO WAR

"We utterly deny all outward wars. . . . The spirit of Christ which leads us into all truth will never move us to fight war against any man . . . therefore we cannot learn war anymore." This is the pledge of some of the first settlers of our nation: the Quakers, who wrote these words to King Charles II in 1660. Other colonists also held religious beliefs that would not allow them to fight in a war.

Quakers, Brethren, and Mennonites, some of the first European colonists to the Americas, stood against war because of their Christian beliefs. Their first test was the conflict between white settlers and Native Americans, when the Puritans persecuted members of the peace churches who would not help build forts to protect against the Indians. Some colonies started allowing Quakers and other peace church mem-

"Most Americans are all for religious freedom—at least until it protects a religion they don't like. Then all bets are off."

—*Charles Haynes, First Amendment scholar*

bers to be exempt from military service in the mid-1600s. Other colonies were less accepting; they fined or put in prison men who refused to help fight or maintain forts.

The first military draft came with the Civil War. All male citizens between the ages of twenty and forty-five had to fight in the army if called. The only exceptions were men who paid the government three hundred dollars. This angered other citizens so much that riots broke out in major cities. The Quakers then convinced Congress to pass the first national law allowing **conscientious objectors** to do alternative service.

CONSCIENTIOUS OBJECTORS IN THE WORLD WARS

During World War I, the United States allowed alternative service assignments only to members of recognized peace churches. Political or social objectors had to join the military if called on to do so, and the military court-martialed five hundred objectors who refused to serve and dealt with them harshly. They sentenced seventeen to death and gave 147 life sentences in prison. The military actually executed no one, and they reduced the life sentences, but the physical abuse these men received was terrible. The army subjected them to solitary confinement, forced exercise, cold showers, and very little food. One young man who refused to wear a uniform caught pneumonia and died. His body was sent home dressed in a uniform.

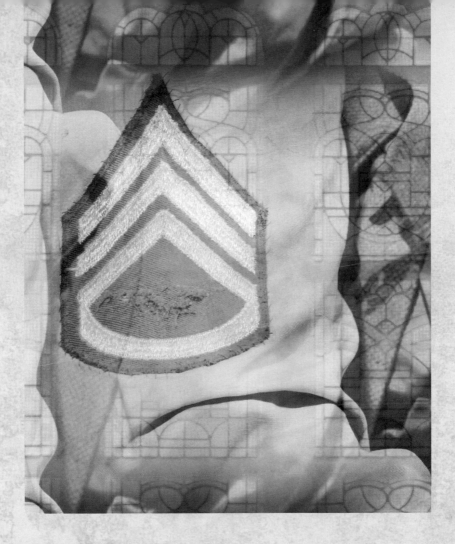

Mennonites, Seventh-Day Adventists, Quakers, Jehovah's Witnesses, Brethren, and members of other peace churches made up most of the World War I conscientious objectors. Most citizens looked on any dissenters as "*subversive radicals*." The government took away their constitutional rights to freedom of speech and assembly, as well as their freedom of the press.

In World War II, the Selective Training and Service Act of 1940 allowed those who objected to war because of religious belief to be exempt from military service. Instead they had to participate in alternative service projects. They worked in mental hospitals, at public service camps, or volunteered to be human guinea pigs in experiments on diet or the

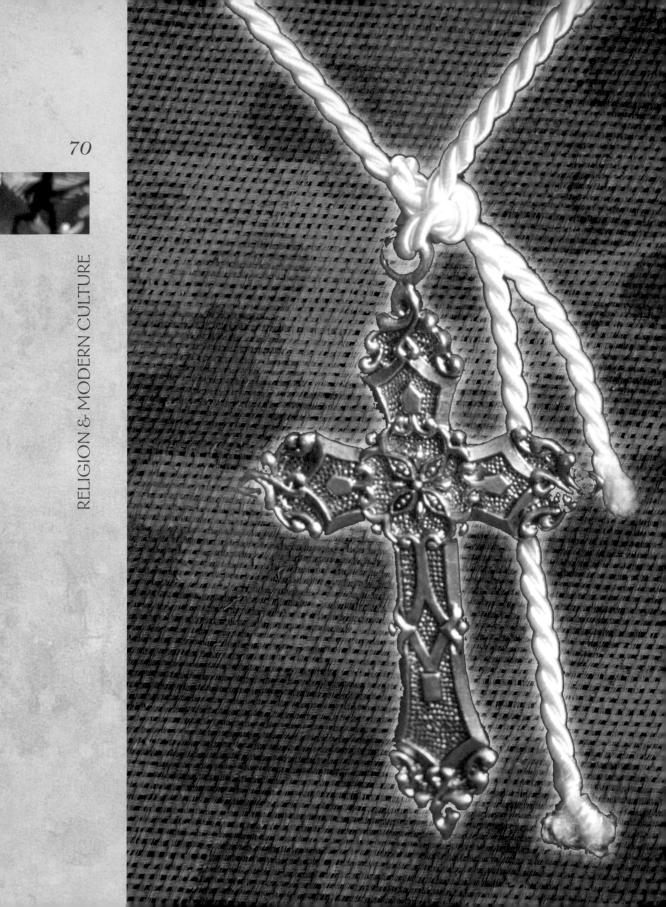

CANADIAN CONSCIENTIOUS OBJECTORS

Canada has a long history of tolerance for conscientious objectors. During the colonial period, Canada encouraged groups such as Mennonites, Quakers, and Brethren in Christ to migrate to Canada, promising they would not have to serve in the military. Canada recognized "scruples of conscience" as well as religious grounds for military exemption.

effects of diseases. They received no pay or benefits and depended on families and churches for financial support.

The Nation of Islam was an African American religious group whose members refused to serve in the military in World War II. They saw the war as a "white man's conflict." About four hundred African Americans refused to serve in the war. They did not want to serve a country that denied them basic freedoms.

THE VIETNAM WAR

During the Vietnam War, the U.S. government granted conscientious-objector status only to religion-based conscientious objectors. Because

> *"The real and lasting victories are those of peace,*
> *and not of war."*
>
> —Ralph Waldo Emerson

the war was unpopular with many people in the United States, political objectors had much public support. In the 1960s, the peace movement became politically powerful. Approximately 50,000 conscientious objectors left the country or assumed false identities, 250,000 never registered for military service, and 110,000 burned their draft cards.

IRAQ WAR

In 2005, the U.S. military still recognizes conscientious objectors. A representative for the Episcopal Peace Fellowship working group on conscientious objectors says he receives a majority of calls from enlisted military personnel. Many of them start to rethink their values and beliefs once they get into a war. It takes about a year for the military to review and decide on applicants for conscientious-objector status.

In 2003, the first conscientious objectors filed for removal from the Iraq War. Camilo Mejia spent eight years in the army and in the Florida National Guard and was in Iraq for seven months. He was home on furlough in October 2003 when he decided that after all he had seen and experienced, he could not in good conscience return to Iraq. He had come to believe the war was illegal and immoral. He turned himself in to the authorities and handed in a fifty-five-page application for conscientious-objector status. The army denied his request. He served a one-year prison term in Oklahoma for desertion.

OBJECTOR GOES NORTH

Brandon Hughey enlisted in the U.S. Army at age seventeen. During his basic training, he educated himself on the Iraq War, and he became alarmed about joining the war. He was so unhappy about going to war that he thought about killing himself.

On the Internet, he met a stranger who offered to help him get to Canada. The night before his scheduled deployment, he drove seventeen hours to meet a peace activist who escorted him across the border, where a Quaker couple took him in. Through their church, he met a lawyer, Jeffry House, who had come to Canada from the United States in 1970 when he was drafted into the military during the Vietnam War. Brandon is applying to Canada for asylum. He plans to argue that under international law the war in Iraq is illegal and that he has a right to choose not to fight.

While the armed services support members in their various religious beliefs, some citizens in the United States contend that their rights to exercise religion are decreasing. Concerns include removal of public Christmas celebrations, laws against posting the Ten Commandments in public places, and challenges to the phrase "under God" in the Pledge of Allegiance.

Chapter 6

RELIGION & MODERN CULTURE

RELIGIOUS SYMBOLS
ON PUBLIC GROUNDS

"O Christmas Tree, O Christmas Tree, Your branches green delight us." What could be more charming, and more cheerful, than a big Christmas tree in a public park—all covered with shining, blinking lights? However, don't look for that big, beautiful Christmas tree in Newport Richey, Florida. In December 2004, county officials ruled all the Christmas trees displayed on public property had to come down. The county attorney claimed the trees were religious symbols. The whole escapade started when a citizen asked the county if he could display a ***menorah*** at a public building.

When the county attorney looked into it, he decided if the town allowed one religious symbol, they had to allow all religious symbols. The county attorney then decided to have no religious symbols at Christmas—and he believed Christmas trees to be religious. The decision upset more than a few local citizens. A lawyer with the American Center for Law & Justice commented that the government legally considers Christmas trees a secular symbol for Christmas.

The Newport Richey Christmas tree decision is just one example of a whole host of issues concerning religious symbols on public grounds. Again, government officials must decide whose freedom and whose faith prevails in a society with diverse beliefs. If a nativity scene or menorah is displayed on public grounds, is the state establishing religion? If such symbols are outlawed on public grounds, is that denying exercise of religion?

CANADIANS FOCUS ON MULTICULTURAL WINTER HOLIDAYS

Religious minorities in Canada during Christmas 2004 were more content. As they drove through holiday landscapes around many towns, they probably noticed fewer Christian symbols than were seen in previous years. Businesses have been careful to include a variety of holiday traditions in their decorations and celebrations recently.

Forest Run Public School in Maple, Ontario, had a variety of music at their holiday program. The children sang songs of Kwanzaa, Christmas, Hanukkah, and the Mexican Las Posada. Their teacher explained the seven principles of Kwanzaa, a festival for people with an African heritage. Another teacher gave a presentation of Diwali, a festival for Hindus and Sikhs celebrated near the end of November. A Christian teacher told students about the birth of baby Jesus. The school understands and supports the idea that people do not have to be the same. Many Canadian citizens see this time of year as a season for entertaining and gift giving rather than as a religious festival.

ISSUES CONCERNING RELIGIOUS SYMBOLS ON PUBLIC GROUNDS IN THE UNITED STATES

Traditionally in the United States, citizens have allowed religious symbols on public property. As the rich diversity of the country has grown, however, so have concerns about these symbols. In communities with varied religions, minorities want to see their religions honored along with majority beliefs. In the early 1990s, federal courts began hearing an increasing number of cases about religious symbols. In 1990, for example, a Superior Court judge in Arizona ruled that the chapel cross at Arizona State University had to come down as it violated the separation of church and state.

Other debates over religious symbols have centered on holiday issues. Communities have seen Christmas, with its religious roots, as

RELIGION & MODERN CULTURE

"Merry Chrismahanakwanzaka to you!"

—multicultural greeting from the 2004 Virgin Mobile phone

commercial

especially controversial. It has long been a legal holiday, though millions of North Americans do not celebrate it. Some believe this shows government favoritism to Christianity.

In Denver, Colorado, "Festival of Lights" organizers banned the Faith Bible Chapel's nativity float, saying that it violated their policy of no overtly religious or political themes. A department store, Boscov's, in Pennsylvania and New York, removed all greeting cards that mentioned Christmas. A number of national stores did away with "Merry Christmas" from their holiday decorations.

The Supreme Court holds that a Christmas tree has become a symbol of the winter holiday season and that it is secular. They also ruled that a Hanukkah menorah is a symbol with both secular and religious significance; as a result, it is legal to place a menorah in public areas other than schools. There is no problem when religious displays are on private property. In some cities, governments have decided that religious displays must only be on private property.

DECISIONS REGARDING THE TEN COMMANDMENTS IN SCHOOLS

Would you like to see a copy of the Ten Commandments in your classroom? Do you feel that would be pushing Jewish or Christian beliefs on students? Would posting the commandments change anyone's behavior in the classroom? Decisions about public display of the commandments have upset some U.S. citizens.

The State of Kentucky passed a law in 1980 that all public schools must display the Ten Commandments in each classroom. Private donations paid for sixteen-by-twenty-inch (41 x 51 centimeters) posters for each class. A group of parents challenged the law, and a state trial followed. The state court ruled in favor of the State of Kentucky: schools could post the Ten Commandment posters. The court decided that the purpose of the posters was "secular and not religious" and that they would not advance or inhibit any religion or religious group.

The case was appealed to the U.S. Supreme Court. In the case known as *Stone v. Graham,* the Court ruled five to four that the Kentucky law was unconstitutional. According to the Court, the posters did not have a secular purpose and had no educational benefit. It did not matter who funded them. Putting them in public classrooms showed government support.

The Supreme Court decided the Ten Commandments are religious in nature and not secular. When a state requires that a religious symbol or teaching be displayed, they are putting the government seal of approval on it. According to the First Amendment, the government may not promote, directly or indirectly, any single religious message.

For many conservative Christians, the removal of the Ten Commandments from public places is an example of America's moral decline. Evangelical radio broadcaster Pat Robertson believes: "Most Americans embrace these commandments as an indispensable part of our nation's moral heritage." He says those who oppose public display of the commandments do so because "the Ten Commandments represent absolute truth, and that cramps their styles." Robertson claims removing the Ten Commandments from public display in the United States will deprive his fellow citizens of "safety, security, peace of mind, and a life free from many troubles."

In 1998, Senator Robert Aderholt introduced the Ten Commandment Defense Act in the House of Representatives. The bill would give individual states—not the federal government—the authority

I
OU SHALT HAVE NO OTHER
GODS BEFORE ME.

II
OU SHALT NOT MAKE UNTO
THEE ANY GRAVEN IMAGE... THOU SHALT
OWN THYSELF TO THEM NOR SERVE THEM.

III
OU SHALT NOT TAKE THE NAME OF
THE LORD THY GOD IN VAIN.

IIII
EMBER THE SABBATH DAY TO KEEP IT
AND HE RESTED THE SEVENTH DAY WHERE
D BLESSED THE SABBATH DAY AND HALLOWED IT.

V
NOR THY FATHER AND THY
THER THAT THY DAYS MAY BE LONG UPON
WHICH THE LORD THY GOD GIVETH THEE.

VI
◼ THOU SHALT NOT KILL.

VII
◼ THOU SHALT NOT COMMIT ADULTERY.

VIII
◼ THOU SHALT NOT STEAL.

IX
◼ THOU SHALT NOT BEAR FALSE
WITNESS AGAINST THY NEIGHBOR.

X
◼ THOU SHALT NOT COVET.

RELIGION & MODERN CULTURE

THOU SHALT NOT POST THE TEN COMMANDMENTS ON PUBLIC GROUNDS

In the 1950s and 1960s, the Fraternal Order of Eagles put up approximately 4,000 Ten Commandment markers in public places. The purpose of this project was to encourage moral, law-abiding behavior. Since the 1980 case of *Stone v. Graham*, there have been lawsuits against a number of states to force the removal of the Ten Commandments from public properties.

to decide whether to display the Ten Commandments on public property. In June 1999, the House of Representatives voted 248 to 180 to add the Ten Commandment Defense Act to a juvenile crime bill. As of January 2005, the bill had not passed in the Senate.

THE PLEDGE OF ALLEGIANCE—UNDER GOD?

"I pledge allegiance to the flag of the United States of America, and to the Republic for which it stands; one nation, *without God*, indivisible with liberty and justice for all." This version of the U.S. Pledge of Allegiance is a *parody* written by an *atheist*. Such a pledge would be offensive to devoutly religious students. Yet atheists allege the current version of the pledge is offensive to them.

In June 2004, the Supreme Court began considering some issues concerning the Pledge of Allegiance. They debated whether it violates students' First Amendment rights to be made to recite the pledge in public schools and whether the phrase "under God," which was added to the pledge in 1954, violates the laws that protect religious freedom.

In 1943, the Supreme Court ruled schools could not force students to say the Pledge of Allegiance. In spite of this ruling, some schools continued to make students say the pledge. In March 1998, school officials made a thirteen-year-old Jehovah's Witness in Seattle stand out in the rain for fifteen minutes because he would not say the pledge. In 2003, the State of Colorado passed a law saying students had to recite the pledge unless they had a written note from their parents; their excuse had to be for religious reasons. The ACLU, along with three students and six teachers, filed a lawsuit against that law and won. District Judge Lewis Babcock wrote, "It doesn't matter whether you're a teacher, a student, a citizen, an administrator, or anyone else, it is beyond the power of the authority of government to compel the recitation of the Pledge of Allegiance."

Michael Newdow, an atheist, agreed it was unconstitutional for his elementary school daughter to have to say the Pledge of Allegiance. He filed a suit, but the federal judge dismissed the case. He took his case to the Ninth Circuit Court of Appeals. They ruled in favor of Newdow in *Newdow v. U.S. Congress.* The justices believed the phrase "under God" showed favoritism toward Christianity and that it was unconstitutional in the school setting. The Ninth Circuit decision conflicted with a previous court decision about the Pledge of Allegiance, so the Supreme Court agreed to hear the case. Newdow, being a physician and a lawyer, argued the case himself before the Supreme Court. In the end, the Court decided that because Newdow did not have physical custody of his daughter—her mother did—he did not have the legal standing to bring the case before the Court. They would not decide on the case.

profiling

Issues concerning the posting of the Ten Commandments or celebration of Christmas can certainly be emotional. Religions—and freedom—are values near and dear to citizens of the United States and Canada. The only thing dearer may be the right to life itself.

The twenty-first century has introduced a new kind of anxiety to residents of the United States—the fear of terrorism. The terrorists who slew thousands of innocent people in the attack on New York's World Trade Center were Muslims, a fact that has caused fears and misunderstandings. Muslims in North America are emphatic that their religion is opposed to terrorism. Yet in the wake of the attacks, there has been a backlash of mistrust toward Muslim communities in the United States. This has led to the very worst violations of religious liberty—religious hate crimes.

Chapter 7

RELIGIOUS HATE CRIMES & PROFILING

The people of the United States will never forget the tragic bombing of the World Trade Center and Pentagon on September 11, 2001, when nearly three thousand innocent people lost their lives. In the weeks following the terrorist attacks, the Arab community, innocent American citizens, felt a backlash of anti-Arab anger. Amnesty International reported that 540 attacks occurred in the week following September 11.

According to the Council on Islamic Relations, most of the crimes were in the form of hate mail, attacks on physical property, and physical assaults. Places of worship—mosques and Hindu temples—were vandalized. Perhaps saddest of all was the killing of an innocent man, Balbir Singh Sodhi.

The Sodhi family had arrived in the United States in the 1980s. They came to pursue the "American Dream," and they worked hard driving cabs, managing gas stations, and working in restaurants. In the years before the September 11 attacks, the family did not experience any prejudice, but immediately after, they sensed trouble.

Balbir, the oldest brother, lived in Mesa, outside Phoenix, Arizona. On September 15, 2001, he drove to Costco to buy an American flag. He wanted to display it at the gas station he had bought nine months earlier. On his way out of the store, he stopped and donated seventy-five dollars to the 9/11 victim's fund. Later that afternoon, he was stooping over planting flowers when a man in a pickup truck pulled into the gas station, shot him, and sped off. The Phoenix man accused of killing Balbir said he shot him because he was dark skinned, had a beard, and was wearing a turban. Less than a year later, the Sodhi family received a crushing second blow. One of Balbir's younger brothers, Sukhpal, was shot and killed while driving a cab at four in the morning. The San Francisco police have not made any arrests in the case. They are not certain what the motive for the crime was, but the Sodhi family thinks they know. The Sodhis are Sikhs, and Sikh men wear turbans—which means they are sometimes mistaken for Muslims, and like Muslims, they are targeted for racial and religious hate crimes.

The Sodhi family suffered terribly through the two tragedies. Nonetheless, a younger brother, Lakhwinder, feels that something special came out of the murders when members of the community arranged a memorial service. Four thousand people of all ages and faiths came to speak out against hate. The brother believes that perhaps the murders have helped people realize Sikhs and Muslims are much like everyone

GLOSSARY

imams: Men who lead prayers in a mosque.

pluralistic: Allowing many ethnic and religious groups equal participation.

Qur'an: The Muslim holy scriptures; also spelled Koran.

stereotypes: Simplified images applied to all individuals within a group, based on prejudice and ignorance.

else under their turbans, beards, and dark skin. If more understanding comes from this, then perhaps his brothers' deaths may save others.

RELIGIOUS TERRORISM IN AMERICA: THE CENTURY-LONG TRAGEDY OF THE KU KLUX KLAN

People who consider Islam a "religion of terror" would be wise to recall Christianity had its own "terror squad" that began in the United States a century ago.

General Nathan Bedford Forrest, a Southern Civil War general, founded the Ku Klux Klan (KKK) in 1865. The group claimed to be a religious brotherhood. Wearing masks, white cardboard hats, and white sheets, they came in the middle of the night to torture and kill blacks,

> *"Do not let hatred of a people incite you to aggression."*
> —*The Holy Qur'an, Surah 5:2*

white supporters of blacks, and immigrants. Congress passed the Ku Klux Act in 1871, which gave the president power to fight against the KKK.

A second Ku Klux Klan formed outside Atlanta, Georgia, in 1915, started by William J. Simmons. Four million people joined the KKK by its peak in the 1920s. Among the members were state officials from Texas, Oklahoma, Indiana, Oregon, and Maine. The group preached racism against immigrants, Roman Catholics, Jews, blacks, socialists, and communists. Hate crimes toward blacks in the South erupted again in the 1960s and continued into the 1980s. Finally, in the later years, states sentenced some KKK members to life in prison, and one man received the death penalty for the murder of an African American.

Once America's number-one terrorist group, the KKK is now a splintered collection of small groups and individuals. Most young white supremacists think of Klansmen as old timers. Regrettably, the United States is not free from racial and religious hate crimes. They have just taken new forms.

SEPTEMBER 11, 2001—TERRORISM BECOMES ASSOCIATED WITH ISLAM BY SOME U.S. CITIZENS

The brother of murder victim Balbir has a little boy. After his two uncles were murdered, the little boy asked his dad, "Why are people shooting at my family?" There's no good answer.

The FBI's annual Hate Crime Report stated that in the year after the World Trade Center event, hate crimes against people and places associated with Islam jumped from 28 in 2000 to 481 in 2001. Some people in the United States immediately began to associate terrorists with those of the Islamic faith around them.

Nehad Awad, the director of the Council on American Islamic Relations (CAIR), spoke out against the terrorists, saying terrorists had hijacked Islam to justify their terrible acts. The men who flew into the New York towers are not from the United States' Muslim community. Awad says they took the name of their faith—they stole it from them—and he is horrified that the perpetrators twisted the text of the *Qur'an* to justify their acts.

ISLAM: "NO COMPULSION IN RELIGION"

Why is violence so often associated with Islam? Professor Jamal Badawi says:

Jihad [holy war] cannot be connected with senseless terrorism. One of the greatest myths is that there is anything in [our] scriptures equivalent to Holy War. I would challenge anyone to find an instance of the term holy war in the Qur'an.

He goes on to explain that Jihad means effort, exertion, and excellence. The Qur'an says to "make Jihad with the Qur'an," not with the sword. Islam allows making Jihad with the sword only under two circumstances: for self-defense and for fighting oppression.

Imams also teach that there should be no compulsion in religion. This is according to Surah 10:99 in the Holy Qur'an. That verse says Allah does not force people to believe—and neither should followers of Islam.

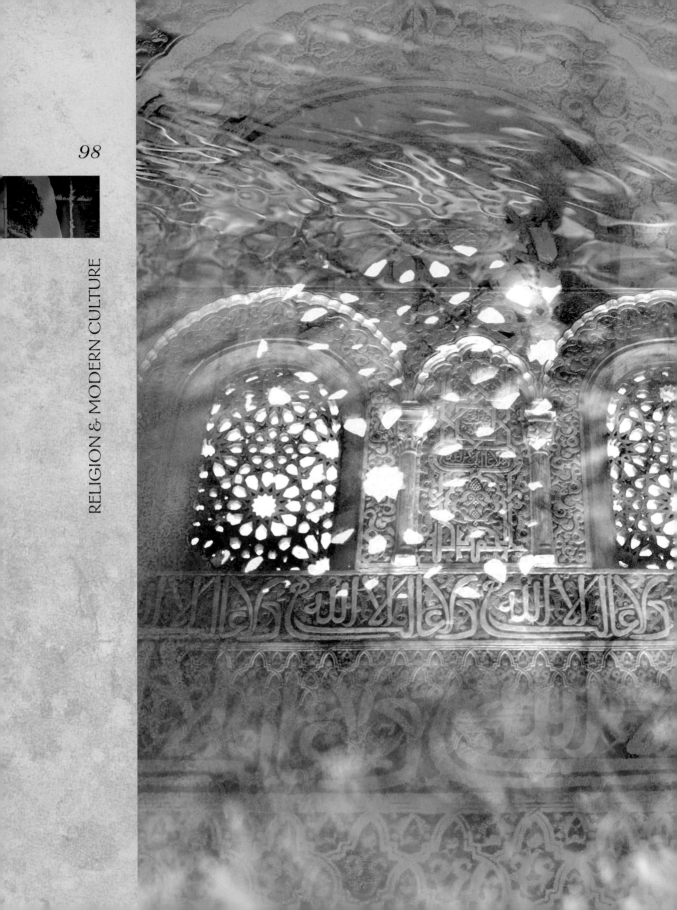

RELIGION & MODERN CULTURE

THE MEANING OF ISLAM

Jamal Badawi, a professor at a university in Halifax, Nova Scotia, explains the meaning of Islam in Diana Eck's book *A New Religious America:* Islam, he says, means peace, submission, and commitment. One gets peace through submission to God and commitment to God.

Allah is the Arabic word for God. Christians who speak Arabic also call God *Allah*, just as the French worship *Dieu*, and Germans worship *Gott*.

On an Oprah Winfrey show called "Islam 101," Oprah interviewed an Arab woman named Manal who had a few things she wanted her American neighbors to know about Islam. She explained Muslims are not so different from other people; Islam does not preach violence. She ended by saying:

Islam and Christianity and Judaism, and all the world's religions share a common heritage. We come from the same root. And our prophets and the characters in our holy books are the same. In Islam, all the religions are permitted to exist in peace with these others until Judgment Day.

"Our diversity is a godsend for us, and the world of the twenty-first century. But it is also the potential for the old, haunting demons that are hard to root out of the human spirit."
—Former President Bill Clinton

RELIGIOUS & ETHNIC PROFILING

The U.S. government has detained many young Middle Eastern male immigrants since the September 11 attacks. Then-attorney general John Ashcroft asked police chiefs around the country to help round up five to ten thousand young Middle Eastern men. The government wanted to find out if they knew anything about the attacks.

Profiling is the practice of singling out persons as suspects for a crime based on their race, country of origin, or religion. Some government officials believe profiling is justified to combat terrorism. Others believe profiling violates civil liberties.

In the first weeks after the profiling began, the FBI and the Immigration and Naturalization Service (INS; now the U.S. Citizenship and Immigration Services) detained over 1,200 Arabs, South Asians, Sikhs, and Muslims. Authorities charged only one man in connection with the September 11 attacks. As of 2002, the government had still detained over three hundred of this group. Authorities have not released names of those detained, the specific crimes with which they are charged, or where they are being held. Officials have released the others. Some have been deported or are awaiting deportation. Those still imprisoned say the government is detaining many more. According to the National Network for Immigrant and Refugee Rights, as of 2002, officials were possibly holding as many as two thousand in another group, and the FBI forced five thousand newly arrived male Arab immigrants

to "volunteer" for questioning. Arnold Garcia, of Network News for Immigrants and Refugee Rights Web site, condemns these actions; all immigrants should have constitutional and civil rights. He comments, "No nation of immigrants would treat immigrants this way."

Those in favor of ethnic and racial profiling believe it is an acceptable practice in times of war. Bruce J. Terris expresses this view in the book *Civil Liberties* by John Derbyshire. He thinks that because of the events of September 11, the United States cannot afford to *not* check on the public. He writes that during passenger screenings before boarding airplanes, it is a waste of time to check on eighty-year-old ladies and eight-year-old children. Terris believes "if experts establish rational profiling criteria, we can concentrate our efforts on the categories of passengers likely to be dangerous."

HATE CRIMES AGAINST MUSLIMS & MEMBERS OF OTHER EASTERN RELIGIONS IN RECENT YEARS

The U.S. Department of Justice has recorded a steady rise in hate crimes during the last few years. Race-related crimes are the highest; next are religion-related crimes. Unfortunately, the sharp rise in hate crimes after 9/11 has not stopped. According to the Council on American-Islamic Relations, a Washington, D.C., Islamic civil rights group, there were one thousand cases of hate crimes in 2004, up from six hundred in 2003. After the 2004 beheading of Paul Johnson Jr. in Saudi Arabia, hate crimes again increased against Muslims. Days after the murder, vandals outside Tampa, Florida, broke the windows of an Islamic center and wrote on the walls, "Kill All Muslims." In Hollywood, Florida, someone left a similar note inside a mosque. In Leon County, Florida, one man drove his truck into an Islamic center, causing thousands of dollars in damage.

Naielah, the president of the Muslim Student Association at her college, has not been the victim of a hate crime, but she takes no chances. Since September 11, 2001, she never goes out after ten o'clock, and she does not travel alone in the evening. When she wears her traditional headdress, a hijab, she often feels the cold stares of people. She realizes this distrust is prompted because of ignorance. Too many United States citizens are not educated about Islam and have many *stereotypes*.

CANADIAN HATE CRIMES

The Canadian Center for Justice Statistics worked with twelve major police departments to conduct a survey on hate crimes in Canada between 2001 and 2002. During that time, citizens reported 928 hate crimes. Fifty-seven percent of these were anti-race or ethnic crimes. Forty-three percent were religious hate crimes. Most of the religious hate crimes were against Jewish people; the next largest were against Muslims.

Immediately after September 11, 2001, Canada also experienced a rise in hate crimes. Police associated 15 percent of the crimes at this time to that event. The increase lasted only two months, and about 30 percent of the incidents were directed against Muslims. The Canadian Islamic Congress (CIC), however, thinks some police stations are not keeping accurate records of hate crimes against Muslims. The CIC recorded eleven crimes the year before the 2001 terrorist attacks. After the terrorist event, 173 crimes occurred. This was a 1600 percent rise in crime. Some of these crimes were committed against people who only *looked* Muslim. Sometimes they occurred against buildings mistaken for Muslim mosques. Wahida Valiante, the CIC president, says:

Hate-motivated crimes are the worst. They are against Canadian and Islamic values, regardless of who the victim is, or how serious the offense is judged to be. Hate crimes have been proven to leave deep psychological scars.

THE ONGOING STRUGGLE TO LIVE THE IDEALS OF RELIGIOUS FREEDOM

The men who wrote the Constitution of the United States of America and the Constitution of Canada could not have imagined the religious diversity of the people who would come to live in their countries. The framers of both constitutions gave their people a strong foundation with the promise of religious freedom. Citizens must always work to guard these foundations. People of faith in Canada and the United States have made great strides on the way to a truly *pluralistic* North America, but much remains to be done. The road ahead may still be rocky as people learn how to be different—together.

Balmer, Randall. *Religion in American Life: Religion in Twentieth Century America.* New York: Oxford University Press Inc., 2001.

Eck, Diana L. *A New Religious America: How a "Christian Country" Has Become the World's Most Religiously Diverse Nation.* New York: Harper San Francisco, 2001.

Elias, Jamal J. (adapted by Nancy D. Lewis.) *The Pocket Idiot's Guide to Islam.* Indianapolis, Ind.: Laurence King, 2003.

Freedman, Russell. *In Defense of Liberty: The Story of America's Bill of Rights.* New York: Holiday House, 2003.

Gay, Kathlyn. *Church and State: Government and Religion in the United States.* Brookfield, Conn.: Millbrook Press, 1992.

McIntosh, Kenneth. *Women in North America's Religious World.* Broomall, Pa.: Mason Crest Publishers, 2005.

McIntosh, Kenneth. *The Growth of North American Religious Beliefs: Spiritual Diversity.* Broomall, Pa.: Mason Crest Publishers, 2006.

Ojeda, Auriana. *Civil Liberties: Opposing Viewpoints.* Farmington Hills, Mich.: Green Haven Press, 2004.

Robertson, Pat. *The Ten Offenses: Reclaim the Blessings of the Ten Commandments.* Nashville, Tenn.: Integrity Publishers, 2004.

FOR MORE INFORMATION

ACLU
(American Civil Liberties Union)
www.aclu.org

Canadian Islamic Congress
www.canadianislamiccongress.com/
mc/media_communique.php?
mcdate=2003-03-10

CNN
www.cnn.com

Houghton Mifflin
college.hmco.com/history/
readerscomp/index.html

National Network for Immigrant
and Refugee Rights—
Network News
www.nnirr.org/news/
archived_netnews/no_nation.htm

Ontario Consultants
on Religious Tolerance
www.religioustolerance.org/
welcome.htm#new

Sound Vision—Islamic
Information and Products
www.soundvision.com

U.S. Government
Resources/Information
usgovinfo.about.com

Publisher's note:
The Web sites listed on this page were active at the time of publication. The publisher is not responsible for Web sites that have changed their addresses or discontinued operation since the date of publication. The publisher will review and update the Web-site list upon each reprint.

PICTURE CREDITS

The illustrations in RELIGION AND MODERN CULTURE are photo montages made by Dianne Hodack. They are a combination of her original mixed-media paintings and collages, the photography of Benjamin Stewart, various historical public-domain artwork, and other royalty-free photography collections.

Elio Vilva, Cuban Art Space, Center for Cuban Studies, NY: pp. 8, 9, 110, 111

AUTHORS: Kenneth and Marsha McIntosh are both former teachers. They have two teen children, Jonathan, and Eirené. Marsha has a Bachelor of Science degree in Bible and Education, and Kenneth has a bachelor's degree in English and a master's degree in theology. They live in Flagstaff, Arizona, with their children, a dog, two cats, and two lovebirds. Marsha has worked over the years as a teacher and administrator in programs for Mexican American, Central American, Caribbean, and Cambodian immigrants. She has also served as translator for charitable groups working in Honduras and Peru. Kenneth has served as pastor for three different churches, and has benefited over the years from his conversations and relationships with a Muslim Imam, American Indian spiritual leaders, Buddhists, Hindus, Jews, members from a wide variety of Christian groups, and other people of faith. He is also the author of *Women in North America's Religions* and *People of Faith and Vision: the Latino Religious Experience.*

CONSULTANT: Dr. Marcus J. Borg is the Hundere Distinguished Professor of Religion and Culture in the Philosophy Department at Oregon State University. Dr. Borg is past president of the Anglican Association of Biblical Scholars. Internationally known as a biblical and Jesus scholar, the *New York Times* called him "a leading figure among this generation of Jesus scholars." He is the author of twelve books, which have been translated into eight languages. Among them are *The Heart of Christianity: Rediscovering a Life of Faith* (2003) and *Meeting Jesus Again for the First Time* (1994), the best-selling book by a contemporary Jesus scholar.

CONSULTANT: Dr. Robert K. Johnston is Professor of Theology and Culture at Fuller Theological Seminary in Pasadena, California, having served previously as Provost of North Park University and as a faculty member of Western Kentucky University. The author or editor of thirteen books and twenty-five book chapters (including *The Christian at Play*, 1983; *The Variety of American Evangelicalism*, 1991; *Reel Spirituality: Theology and Film in Dialogue*, 2000; *Life Is Not Work/Work Is Not Life: Simple Reminders for Finding Balance in a 24/7 World*, 2000; *Finding God in the Movies: 33 Films of Reel Faith*, 2004; and *Useless Beauty: Ecclesiastes Through the Lens of Contemporary Film*, 2004), Johnston is the immediate past president of the American Theological Society, an ordained Protestant minister, and an avid bodysurfer.